nest

eggs

beak

wings

feet

tail

swallow

blue tit

robin

sparrow

Can you see
the birds outside?

Birds build nests
in the spring.

Mother bird lays eggs
in the nest.

Mother and father bird sit
on the eggs to keep them warm.

The baby birds
hatch from the eggs.

Mother and father bird
feed the baby birds.

The baby birds grow up.

They learn to fly.

In the autumn
some birds fly away.

Some fly

across the sea.

They fly
to warmer lands.

In the snow
birds cannot always find food.

We can feed the birds
in winter.

Here are some things

birds like to eat.

We keep some birds as pets.

Text © 1971 P Nash Illustrations © 1971 Macmillan Education Ltd
First published 1971 Reprinted 1972, 1973, 1976, 1977, 1978, 1979, 1982
Published by Macmillan Education Ltd Printed in Hong Kong by Dah Hua Printing Press Co., Ltd.